HEALTHY BODY
Exercise

Text by Carol Ballard • Photography by Robert Pickett

BLACKBIRCH®
PRESS

THOMSON
＊
GALE

San Diego • Detroit • New York • San Francisco • Cleveland • New Haven, Conn. • Waterville, Maine • London • Munich

TITLES IN THE HEALTHY BODY SERIES:

• Personal Hygiene • Eating Right • Safety
• Exercise • Relationships • Harmful Substances

© 2004 by White-Thompson Publishing Ltd.

Produced by White-Thompson Publishing Ltd.
2/3 St. Andrew's Place
Lewes BN7 1UP, U.K.

For more information, contact
The Gale Group, Inc.
27500 Drake Rd.
Farmington Hills, MI 48331-3535
Or you can visit our Internet site at http://www.gale.com

Editor:	Elaine Fuoco-Lang
Consultant:	Chris Sculthorpe, East Sussex, Brighton & Hove Healthy School Scheme Co-ordinator
Inside design:	Joelle Wheelwright
Cover design:	Hodder Wayland
Photographs:	Robert Pickett
Proofreader:	Alison Cooper
Artwork:	Peter Bull

Acknowledgements:
The publishers would like to thank the following for their assistance with this book: the staff and children of Whitstable Junior School, Whitstable, Kent, UK.

Originally published by Hodder Wayland, an imprint of Hodder Children's Books, a division of Hodder Headline Limited 338 Euston Road, London NW1 3BH

Picture acknowledgements:
CORBIS 14, Jim Cummins Studio, Inc./CORBIS 9 top, R.W. Jones/CORBIS 7, Cabaret Philippe 12 top, Bill Ross/CORBIS 12 bottom, Pete Saloutos/CORBIS 27 bottom, Tom Stewart Photography/CORBIS 28; Hodder Wayland Picture Library 6 top, 13 top, 25 top; Robert Pickett 4, 5, 6 bottom, 8, 9 bottom, 10 top, 11, 13 bottom, 15, 16, 17, 18, 19, 20, 21, 23, 25 bottom, 27 top, 29; WTPix 10 bottom, 22, 24, 26.

The photographs in this book are of models who have granted their permission for their use in this title.

LIBRARY OF CONGRESS CATALOGING-IN-PUBLICATION DATA

Ballard, Carol.
  Exercise / by Carol Ballard.
    p. cm. — (Healthy body)
Includes bibliographical references and index.
Contents: What is exercise?— Why exercise?—Dressed for action!—Warming up!—Stamina, strength, or speed?—Muscles—Exercising your heart—Temperature control—Energy balance—All in the mind—Do not overdo it!—Drugs and sports—Avoiding accidents and injuries.
  ISBN 1-4103-0157-5 (hardback)
  1. Exercise—Juvenile literature. [1. Exercise. 2. Health.] I. Title. II. Series: Ballard, Carol. Healthy body.
  RA781.B227 2004
  613.7'1—dc22

2003012019

Printed in China
10 9 8 7 6 5 4 3 2 1

Contents

What is exercise?

Exercise is any activity that makes your body work harder than it does when you are just sitting still and relaxing. Some types of exercise, like walking slowly, are gentle. They do not make your body work very hard at all. Other types of exercise, such as competitive swimming, can make your body work very hard indeed.

▶ *There are many different things you can do to give your body a workout.*

You can do some types of exercise, like riding a bike or walking, on your own or with a small group. Other types of exercise, such as team sports like football and basketball, are more organized. They may need more people and equipment and a special place to play.

◀ *Team sports with friends are fun and a great way to exercise.*

All sorts of people can enjoy exercise! You do not have to be young and fit. Many elderly people are very active and take part in different activities. There are all sorts of sports organized for people with a wide range of disabilities. Special athletics events are held for disabled athletes. Some of these athletes achieve great success despite their disabilities.

When we exercise, it is not only good for our bodies, it also makes us feel good about ourselves.

▲ *The more you run, the harder your body has to work.*

Why exercise?

One of the best reasons to exercise is that it is fun! Choose an activity you enjoy and make your body do some work!

Different types of exercise help you to be better at all sorts of things. Some activities can increase your strength. Others increase your speed, agility, flexibility, and stamina. Exercising can improve your coordination so that all parts of your body work well together.

► *Stretching and bending in gymnastics makes your body more flexible.*

Exercise is good for your health. It helps keep your heart strong and healthy, so that it pumps blood efficiently around your body. It helps to keep your lungs working smoothly, too.

Exercise is a good way to relax. While your bones and muscles are working hard, your brain can unwind.

◄ *Running and sprinting use up lots of energy.*

▲ *Tennis is good for improving coordination.*

Your body uses energy all the time, but the more active you are, the more energy it uses. This means that exercise can help people keep their weight under control. Doctors often advise people who are overweight to exercise to help them lose some weight.

!?/ Fantastic Facts

Exercise is so important that astronauts use special equipment so that they can exercise in space. They might run on a treadmill or ride an exercise bike. Because there is no gravity, their exercises are easier to do in space than they are on Earth. Their bones and muscles do not have to work so hard, so their bones slowly become weaker. If they did not exercise, the loss of strength would be even greater.

Dressed for action!

Different activities need different clothes. You can wear your ordinary clothes for some activities, such as playing in the park or going for a walk. For others, though, it is important to wear the right clothing.

Clothing

Some activities can be dangerous, so it makes sense to wear anything that might protect you. You should always wear a helmet when riding your bike. Wear protective pads for knees and elbows when skateboarding or in-line skating. Some team games, such as football, have their own special protective clothing. Make sure you wear it to avoid injury.

▼ *Body pads, gloves, helmets, and face guards all help protect football players.*

Jewelry can be dangerous in some activities. Long, dangly earrings can easily get pulled or caught during gymnastics, for example. You can avoid these dangers by simply not wearing jewelry when you do something active.

Healthy Hints

It is fun to take part in outdoor activities on a warm, sunny day. Remember that too much sun can be dangerous, though. Avoid being in bright sunshine at midday, when the sun's rays are at their strongest. Put sunscreen on all exposed parts of your body to keep your skin from burning. Cover up with a loose T-shirt. Wear a hat or cap to protect your head.

▶ *Always drink water after you have exercised, especially on a hot day.*

Footwear

You use your feet for most activities, so the correct footwear is important. Some sports, such as ice skating, need special footwear. Some sports have special rules about footwear. For example, baseball cleats usually cannot be worn in a soccer game. Fashion footwear may look great, but is not usually sensible for sports. You will do better if you wear shoes that are appropriate for the activity that you are doing.

▶ *When you are playing sports, make sure that you wear appropriate clothing.*

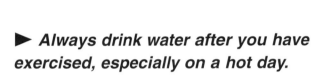

Warming up!

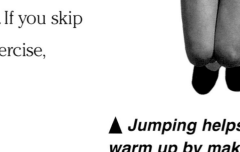

Whether you are a track athlete, swimmer, football player, or dancer, it is important to warm up before you begin. This means making gentle movements to prepare your body for the exercise you are about to do.

Warming up does just what it says—it raises the temperature of your muscles. After a few minutes of warming up, your muscles and joints will be warm and flexible. If you skip the warm-up and go straight into vigorous exercise, you are much more likely to injure yourself.

▲ *Jumping helps you warm up by making your heart work harder.*

▼ *Whatever sport you choose to do, remember to warm up first.*

Warming up is all about getting your whole body ready for exercise. Gentle twisting around your waist and circling your arms will help loosen up your upper body. Stretching exercises help get muscles ready to move quickly.

After some loosening and stretching, try gentle jogging, running in place, jumping, or skipping. These all help make your heart beat faster and prepare your body for more vigorous exercise.

◀ *Stretching helps to warm up your muscles.*

Fantastic Facts

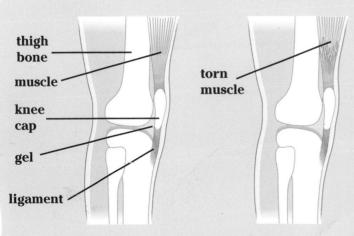

thigh bone

muscle

knee cap

gel

ligament

torn muscle

• Joints contain a gel to help them move smoothly. The warmer you are, the runnier this gel becomes—so the more easily your joints can move.

• When muscles are cold, they are not very elastic. You can easily overstretch them and tear some of the muscle fibers.

◀ *Tearing a muscle is painful. You can keep this from happening by warming up before you exercise.*

Stamina, strength, or speed?

Different types of exercise are good for developing different kinds of skills. To be good at some sports, you may need all of these skills. For others, you may need only some of them.

► *Bicyclists in the Tour de France compete for many days and have to have great stamina.*

◄ *Swimming relies on speed and stamina.*

Exercises such as running, cycling, and swimming make your heart and lungs work hard. Exercises like this are good for building up your stamina, so that you increase the length of time you can exercise without getting tired. They also help increase your speed.

Exercises such as weightlifting and yoga may make your heart and lungs work hard, but they do more as well. Weightlifting can help muscles become stronger. (Be careful, though—weightlifting before your bones are fully grown can keep you from growing and developing properly.) Yoga can increase your flexibility and balance.

Many people combine both types of exercise. This mixture of exercises, together with periods of resting, is called interval training. It is a good way to develop a wide range of skills and make sure every part of you is as fit as possible.

◀ *Yoga is good for flexibility.*

\!?/ Fantastic Facts

There are two types of muscle fibers, each good at a different job. Fast twitch fibers are good for short, sharp bursts of activity. They tire quickly, however, and cannot keep working for a long period. Slow twitch fibers cannot give a sharp burst of activity, but they are able to keep working for a long time without tiring. Fast twitch fibers would help a sprinter, and slow twitch fibers would help a long-distance runner.

▲ *Sprinting helps develop your speed.*

Muscles

The muscles in your body work together in groups. Different activities use different groups of muscles. For example, bicycling needs strong leg muscles. Rowing needs strong arm and shoulder muscles.

Muscle groups

One of the important muscle groups is the abdominal muscles that run in layers up and down and from side to side of the front of your body. Your arms and shoulder movements are controlled by a group of strong muscles anchored to your spine, rib cage, shoulder blade, and collarbones.

A group of muscles anchored to your spine and pelvis allows you to move your legs.

▼ **Strong muscles help these rowers to row fast.**

Muscles that move your body are attached to bones and work in pairs. When one muscle contracts (gets shorter), it stretches the other muscle. When the stretched muscle contracts, the other muscle gets stretched. By contracting, the muscles pull bones into new positions.

Moving your arm

You can see how this works with your arm. As the biceps muscle contracts, it pulls the lower arm up and stretches the triceps muscle. The opposite happens to lower the arm. The triceps contracts, pulling the lower arm down and stretching the biceps.

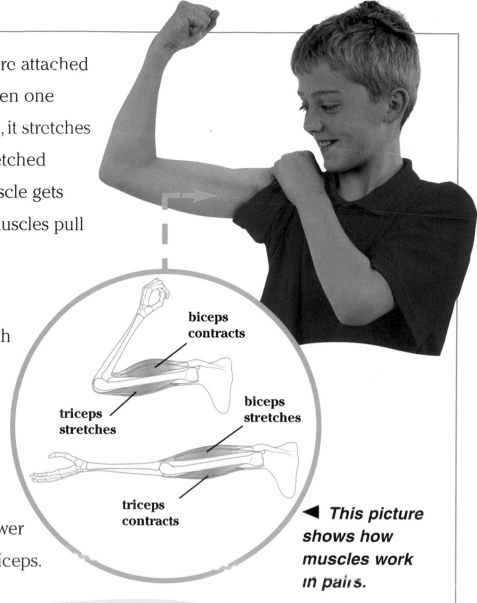

biceps contracts

triceps stretches

biceps stretches

triceps contracts

◄ *This picture shows how muscles work in pairs.*

Action Zone

Put a book on the palm of your hand with your arm stretched out in front of you. Put your other hand on the front of your upper arm. Raise the lower arm and the hand with the book on it. Can your other hand feel your upper arm muscles moving?

▶ *It is easy to feel your muscles moving.*

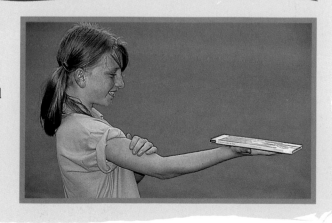

Exercising your heart

Your heart is a very important muscle. It beats every minute of every day. Whether you are awake or asleep, it pumps blood to every part of your body.

● Muscles need energy to move. Your body gets energy from the food that you eat and stores it in a chemical called glucose. To use this stored energy, muscles need oxygen.

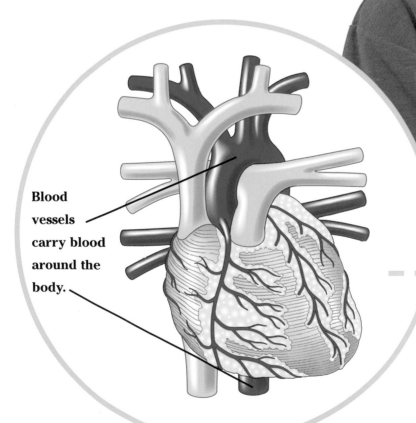

Blood vessels carry blood around the body.

▲ *Place a hand on your chest to feel your heartbeat.*

• Blood brings glucose and oxygen to your muscles. When your muscles work hard, they need more energy and oxygen. So your heart beats faster to pump blood around your body more quickly. After exercise, your muscles need less energy and oxygen. So your heartbeat gradually slows down until it is back to normal again.

• Doing exercise that makes your heart beat faster four or five times a week will help keep your heart fit and strong. If you do not do much exercise, begin slowly. Try to do one or two activities for a couple of weeks, and then slowly build up. You might choose swimming, bicycling, running, dancing, or ball games.

Action Zone

• Put two fingers gently on your wrist, in line with your thumb bone.

• Can you feel your pulse?

• Count how many beats there are in one minute.

• Now jump up and down for two minutes.

• Find your pulse again and count the beats in one minute.

• Were there more beats this time? Can you explain why?

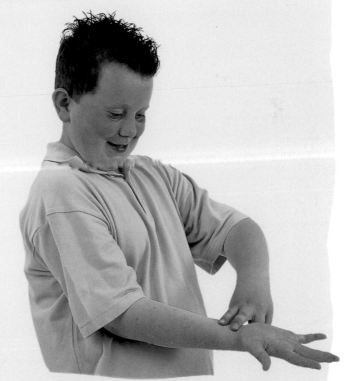

▲ *When you take your pulse, use your fingers, not your thumb.*

Temperature control

When your muscles work, they produce heat. This means that your body gets warmer, but you do not just get hotter ...and hotter ...and hotter! Your body has some very efficient ways to keep you from getting too hot.

Sweating

When your body starts to get hot, tiny pores in the skin allow a salty liquid called sweat to trickle out onto the surface of the skin. As the sweat evaporates into the air, it cools the skin down. When you stop exercising and cool down, your skin stops releasing sweat. It is important to drink plenty of water before, during, and after your activity. This replaces what you lose as you sweat.

▼ *Wearing sweatbands can keep sweat away from your hands.*

◀ *You feel thirsty after exercise because your body loses water in sweat.*

Keeping cool

Blood plays a part in keeping you cool, too. When you are hot, tiny blood vessels near the surface of the skin open a little to allow more blood to pass through them. As the blood passes close to the surface of the skin, it cools down. When you get cold, the opposite happens. The blood vessels become narrower, so less blood passes through to keep any more heat from being lost.

▶ **After you have exercised, your face may look red.**

 # Healthy Hints

When you stop exercising, your body does not stop producing sweat right away, and the tiny blood vessels cannot narrow immediately. This means that you continue to cool down, even though your muscles are not producing any more heat. In a cool climate, you may cool down too much. To keep this from happening, remember to cover up with a tracksuit or something similar as soon as you finish your activity.

◀ **Putting a tracksuit on over exercise clothing will help you avoid overcooling.**

Energy balance

Doing any sort of activity needs energy. Your energy comes from the food that you eat. It is important to make sure that you eat plenty of energy-rich foods, as well as other foods to help your body grow strong and healthy.

Sugar

Foods such as candy, cookies, and sodas contain a lot of sugar. They give you short, quick bursts of energy, but too many sugary foods are bad for your teeth.

Fat

Foods such as fries, sausages, and chips all contain fat that gives you plenty of energy. It is best not to eat too much fat, though.

Starch

Pasta, bread, potatoes, and rice all contain starch. These help you feel full and provide energy for a long time.

Protein

Meat, eggs, and nuts all contain protein, which helps repair muscles and also helps keep you feeling full. They are ideal, healthy sources of energy.

▼ *Chocolate has a lot of energy. It also has lots of fat and sugar, though, so try not to eat too much of it.*

You need to balance the amount of food you eat with the amount of activity you do. With too much food and not enough activity, you may start to become heavy and sluggish. With too little food and too much activity, you may start to become thin and weak. If you get the balance right, you will be fit and active and have enough energy to do just about anything you want!

▲ *A healthy diet includes plenty of fruits and vegetables.*

▲ *A tuna sandwich is a healthy, energy-giving snack.*

∖!?∕ Fantastic Facts

Before you exercise, you need to make sure your body has a store of energy. This is especially important if your activity is going to last for a long time. Sometimes you just need a quick burst of extra energy. Sports drinks can provide such a burst. They contain a lot of sugar that can be quickly absorbed into your blood and carried to the muscles where it is needed.

All in the mind

Exercise is good for your body—and good for your mind. If you are active, your body will get fitter. You will feel better in other ways, too. Your concentration will improve, and you will feel more alert. Exercise can also cheer you up and make you feel more relaxed and confident.

► *Active sports such as waterskiing are great exercise and great fun, too.*

When you exercise, your brain releases special chemicals called endorphins. These act like powerful drugs inside your body. They can act as painkillers, and they also make you feel happier and more confident. Exercise such as running can make you feel really good inside. People who exercise regularly talk about a "runner's high," which refers to the good feeling they have when they finish exercising.

movement

taste

thought

sight

speech

hearing

▲ *Different parts of your brain control different activities.*

Exercise can help your mind relax, so you forget about things that might have been worrying you. A relaxed mind and tired muscles can help you sleep soundly. Exercise can help improve your concentration on other tasks such as schoolwork. Being more alert can help you succeed in other areas, too. Improving your coordination by doing sports can help you feel more confident and outgoing.

▲ *Exercise is good for concentration.*

 # Fantastic Facts

Exercise can be addictive, just like some drugs. Some people start off doing a sensible amount of exercise. Then they gradually do more and more until they are doing far too much. They become addicted to the endorphins that their brain produces. It becomes very difficult for them to stop overexercising and get back to normal.

◄ *Exercise can help to reduce stress and make you feel less anxious.*

Do not overdo it!

Too much exercise can be bad for your body. Your muscles, bones, and other systems all need a period to recover and rest in between exercise. If you do too much, your body has no chance to recover, and you may start to feel unwell. Also, too much exercise can mean that your performance actually gets worse rather than better.

▶ *Taking time to rest between exercise can improve your performance.*

Healthy Hints

Do you know how much sleep you need? Most adults need seven or eight hours of sleep a night. Most children need a lot more—at least ten or eleven hours.

You can easily figure out whether you are getting enough sleep. Count the hours from the time you go to bed until midnight, then add the time you need to get up in the morning.

▲ *Are you getting enough sleep?*

Examples

1. Go to bed at 8:00 P.M., get up at 7:00 A.M. = 4 + 7 = 11 = enough sleep.

2. Go to bed at 10:00 P.M., get up at 6:00 A.M. = 2 + 6 = 8 = not enough sleep.

Too much exercise can harm your immune system. Your immune system is what keeps you well and prevents you from catching colds and other illnesses. If it is harmed, you are more likely to fall ill. If you are unwell, it is better to take it easy for a few days until you recover. It is hard for your body to cope with an illness and a lot of exercise at the same time.

▼ *It is not a good idea to exercise when you are feeling unwell.*

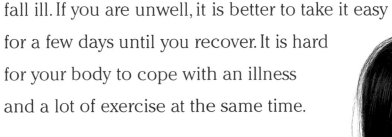

Drugs and sports

Some chemicals can help your body do better at some tasks than it would be able to on its own. Others help your muscles grow stronger than they would naturally. If you were in a competition, this would give you an unfair advantage over people who had not taken these chemicals. Most sports ban competitors from taking any chemicals like this, such as steroids and epinephrine.

Being careful

Athletes have to be very careful because some of these banned substances are found in everyday medicines such as cold and flu remedies. They must read the package carefully and check all the ingredients to make sure they are not taking any banned substances.

▲ *Never be tempted to take drugs to make yourself look different or perform better. Exercising is the best way to keep fit and look good.*

Some young people think that, by taking some of these substances, they will grow stronger and better than their friends and rivals. This is a really bad idea—do not ever be tempted to do it! Some of these substances can have very severe side effects, and may actually prevent your body from growing and developing properly.

Be yourself

Let your body grow naturally. Be pleased that your skills are the result of your own hard work, rather than the result of chemicals.

◀ *If you exercise and eat right, you will look and feel great.*

\\?/ Fantastic Facts

The people in charge of most sports regard taking banned substances as a very serious offense. Scientists have developed sensitive tests that can detect tiny amounts of these substances. At a major competition like the Olympic Games, athletes are tested at random. Anyone found guilty of taking any of the banned substances can face very serious penalties. He or she may even be banned from competing in a sport for the rest of his or her life.

▲ *Winning without chemicals feels great!*

27

Avoiding accidents and injuries

Whatever type of exercise you enjoy, you need to be careful. Remember always to wear the correct protective clothing for your activity. Accidents and injuries can happen, but can often be avoided by taking just a few safety precautions.

▼ *Wearing a helmet when riding a bike will help protect you if you have an accident.*

Going out

If you are going out, make sure an adult knows where you are going, who you are going with, and when you will be back. That way, if you do not get back on time, somebody will know where to look for you and where to send help. If you are going to be out when it is dark, wear reflective clothing.

On the road

If you are walking, remember to stop, look, and listen before you cross a road. If you are bicycling, make sure your bike is in good shape before you set out. Remember to follow all the rules of the road.

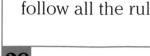

Whatever sport you play, there are rules that should be followed. Many of these are for your own safety and that of the other players. You should try hard to follow them, so that everybody avoids injury.

Think of others

Think about other people who may be exercising near you. Try not to do anything that could hurt them or cause them to feel unsafe in any way. This is especially important if there are younger children around.

▲ *Stretching will help keep you injury free.*

 # Healthy Hints

Just about everybody has suffered from a cramp at some time. It can be very painful, even if it only lasts for a few seconds. A cramp happens when part of a muscle that you can usually control suddenly contracts and does not relax. Rubbing the affected area can sometimes ease the pain. Dehydration can increase the likelihood of getting cramps, so make sure you drink plenty of water.

▼ *Rubbing your foot can help relieve cramps.*

Glossary

abdominal to do with the front of the body, between the ribs and hips.

agility how quickly you are able to move and respond.

biceps the muscle at the front of the upper arm.

blood vessels the tubes through which blood travels around your body.

collarbones the bones at the base of the throat, above the ribcage.

contract get shorter.

coordination how well different parts work together.

dehydration losing fluid through sweating.

energy the power needed to do work.

flexibility how stretchy you are.

glucose a type of sugar that the body uses as a source of energy.

heart the organ that pumps blood around your body.

immune system the body's defense mechanisms that protect you from illness.

joints the places where bones meet.

lungs the organs that collect oxygen from the air and get rid of carbon dioxide when you breathe in and out.

muscles the parts of your body that pull bones to allow you to move.

oxygen a gas in the air that every part of your body needs to work properly.

pelvis the bones that make your hips.

pore a tiny hole.

pulse your heartbeat.

relax become looser.

rib cage the bones of your chest that protect your heart and lungs.

spine your backbone.

stamina how long you can keep doing something before getting tired.

sunscreen cream or lotion that protects you from the harmful rays of the sun.

temperature a measure of how hot or cold something is.

triceps the muscle at the back of the upper arm.

vigorous energetic or hardworking.

For More Information

Gordon, Sharon, *Exercise*. New York: Childrens Press, 2002.

Sadgrove, Judy, *Exercise*. Austin, TX: Raintree Steck-Vaughn, 2000.

Silverstein, Alvin, *Physical Fitness*. New York: Franklin Watts, 2002.

Smithyman, Kathryn, *Active Kids*. New York: Crabtree, 2003.

Vogel, Elizabeth, *Let's Exercise*. New York: PowerKids Press, 2001.

Index